The Bill of Rights

Protecting Our Freedom
Then and Now

The Bill of Rights

Protecting Our Freedom Then and Now

Written by **Syl Sobel**

BARRON'S

Barron's Educational Series, Inc.

*To the students, teachers, and parents of Thurgood Marshall
Elementary School, Gaithersburg, Maryland
Thanks for your encouragement and support!*

Acknowledgments

I wish to thank my colleague, Dr. Bruce Ragsdale, for reviewing this book at several stages and providing valuable suggestions. My wife, Joan, and daughters, Marissa and Isabel, read various versions with critical eyes and offered sound advice. Any errors that may appear in the text are entirely mine.

All inquiries should be addressed to:
Barron's Educational Series, Inc.
250 Wireless Blvd.
Hauppauge, NY 11788
www.barronseduc.com

ISBN: 978-0-7641-4021-1

Library of Congress Catalog Card No. 2008004774

Library of Congress Catalog-in-Publication Data
Sobel, Syl.
    The Bill of Rights: protecting our freedom then and now/ by Syl Sobel.
        p. cm.
    Includes bibliographical references and index.
    ISBN-13: 978-0-7641-4021-1
    ISBN-10: 0-7641-4021-3
  1. United States. Constitution. 1st-10th Amendments—Juvenile
literature.   2. Civil rights—United States—History—Juvenile
Literature.   3. Constitutional amendments—United States—
History—Juvenile literature.   I. Title.

KF4750.S64 2008
342.7308/5 22   2008004774

Date of Manufacture: December 2012
Manufactured by: MO3IO3D, Guangdong, China

9 8 7 6 5 4 3 2

Contents

Introduction

Have you ever heard someone say, "It's a free country?" Do you know what that means?

The people of the United States have many freedoms, which are called *rights*. We have the right to protest the government's decisions and to write articles and go on television to complain about the government. We have the right to practice any religion—or no religion—as we choose. The government cannot just arrest us and throw us in jail for no reason. We have the right to know what crime the government says we committed and to have a fair trial before the government can put us in jail.

All of these rights are protected by the *Bill of Rights*. The Bill of Rights is part of the *Constitution of the United States*. But the Bill of Rights was not in the original Constitution. Many of the people who wrote the Constitution did not think the Bill of Rights was necessary. Why is the Bill of Rights in the Constitution, how did it get there, and what do these rights mean? Let's find out.

A Confederation of States

In 1783, thirteen British colonies in North America won their independence from Great Britain. Gaining their independence required a long and costly war, called the Revolutionary War or the War of Independence. But the colonies, which were now called *states* because they were independent, had more problems ahead of them: How would they survive on their own? Would they continue to do business with England and with other countries in Europe? Would they be safe—from French and Spanish settlements nearby, from Native Americans, from pirates, from each other—without the British army and navy to protect them? What kind of government would they form for their new country?

At first, leaders of the states organized their states into a *confederation*, which is another word for league. The confederation was not very well organized, however. Each state ran like a separate country with its own rules. The confederation had very few rules to make the states work together. Each state had its own type of money and its own army called a *militia*. Each militia, however, only protected its own state. The confederation had no power to raise money for an army and a navy to protect all of the states. The leaders called the confederation the "United States," but the states were not really united yet as one nation.

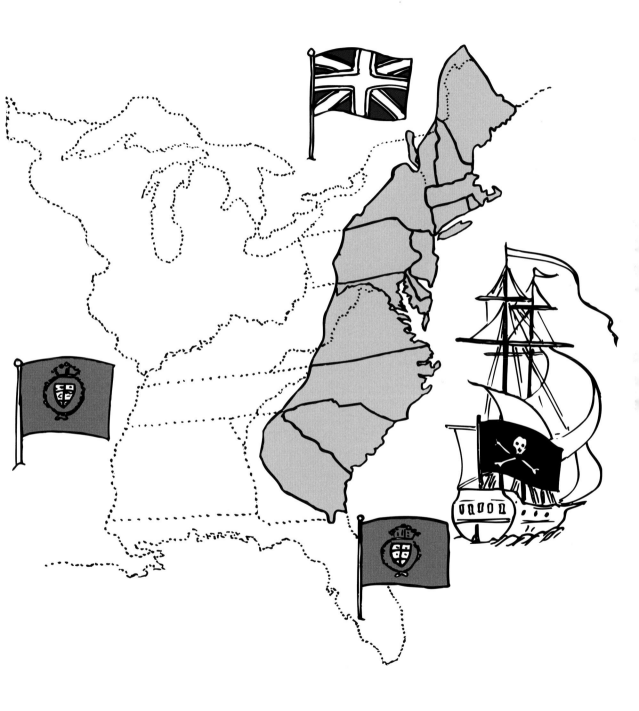

The Constitutional Convention

By 1787, leaders of the states realized that they needed to work together as one country. That summer, all of the states except Rhode Island sent representatives to meet in Philadelphia. The representatives at that meeting decided to create a new government for all of the states, which was called a *national government*, and to write rules for that government. These rules were called the Constitution of the United States, and the meeting was called the *Constitutional Convention*.

We call the people who wrote the Constitution the *Framers* or the *Founders*. The fifty-five Framers at the Constitutional

Convention were smart and well educated. Many of the brightest, most respected, and most important people in the United States at that time were there. The convention took place in the Pennsylvania State House, which was the same place where some of the Framers had met eleven years earlier to approve the Declaration of Independence. That building is now called Independence Hall.

The Framers elected General George Washington of Virginia, the military hero of the Revolutionary War, as president of the convention. James Madison, a small, modest, well-respected member of Congress from Virginia, wrote an initial plan for a constitution and was the convention's secretary. Benjamin

Franklin, the famous writer, publisher, and inventor from Pennsylvania, at age 81, was the elder statesman of the group. Legend has it that sometimes he fell asleep in his chair during long and boring speeches. After all, it was a hot summer in Philadelphia, and the Framers closed the State House windows so that no one outside could hear what they were doing. But notes of the convention, most of them kept by Madison, show that Franklin also offered wise advice at several important moments.

James Madison

John Adams of Massachusetts and Thomas Jefferson of Virginia, two well-known leaders of the Revolution, were not at the convention. Adams was the U.S. minister to England. Jefferson was the U.S. minister to France. They did, however, follow the progress of the convention through letters that some of the Framers wrote to them.

Many Disagreements

The Framers had much in common, but they also had many differences. People from some states did not like people from some other states. For many years, some states had argued over which one owned certain pieces of land or had the right to use certain rivers and lakes. Framers who lived in smaller states were afraid that big states, like Virginia and Massachusetts, would become too powerful in a national government. Framers who lived in big states were afraid of giving too much power to the smaller states, which outnumbered them.

Many Framers disagreed over slavery. Since the early days of the colonies, slaves from Africa were bought and sold, treated as property, and often lived and worked in terrible conditions. By 1787, most slaves lived in the southern states, which depended on slave labor to plant, harvest, and perform other work on large farms called *plantations*. Framers from northern states wanted the Constitution to end slavery, or at least to end the cruel shipment of slaves from Africa, which was called the *slave trade*. Framers from southern states threatened to leave the convention if the Constitution ended slavery or the slave trade. Everyone at the convention knew that without the support of the southern states, a national government would not succeed.

Framers disagreed on how much power to give to the new national government. The states had just fought the War of Independence mainly because they did not like all the power that King George III and the British government had over them. Many Framers worried about creating a new government that could become as powerful as the king's. Some Framers wanted the states to keep most of their powers and the national government to have very little power. Other Framers wanted a strong national government with many powers over the states.

Framers also disagreed on how to organize the new national government. Some Framers wanted the national government to have one powerful leader. Some wanted several leaders to share power. Some wanted to give most of the government's power to *representatives*, whom the people would elect to make rules, called *laws*, for them.

Federalism, Separation of Powers, Checks and Balances, and Other Compromises

With all of these differences, writing the Constitution required the Framers to make deals or *compromises*. With these compromises, one side received some, but not all, of what it wanted, and the other side got some, but not all, of what it wanted.

To compromise between a strong national government and strong state governments, the Framers created a central U.S. government that shared power with state governments. The

Constitution gave the U.S. government power to make some laws for all of the states. It also gave the U.S. government power to raise money by collecting taxes and to organize an army and other military forces. State governments, however, were also allowed to make laws for their citizens, collect taxes, and have other powers. This system of shared power between state and national governments was called *federalism*.

To compromise on how to organize the government, the Framers created a government in which three parts, called *branches*, shared power. The Constitution gave the *legislative branch*, called Congress, power to make laws. It gave the *executive branch*, led by the President, power to carry out the laws and make sure people obeyed the laws. It gave the *judicial branch*, which contained the courts, power to decide whether laws met the Constitution's requirements and to decide other legal questions, such as whether someone broke a law. This system of shared power was called *separation of powers*.

To compromise between the large and small states, the Framers split the legislative branch into two parts, called *houses*. The Constitution gave one house, the *Senate*, two members from each state. That way every state, no matter how big or small, had the same number of votes in the Senate. In the other house, the *House of Representatives*, the number of members from each state depended on how many people lived in the state. Larger

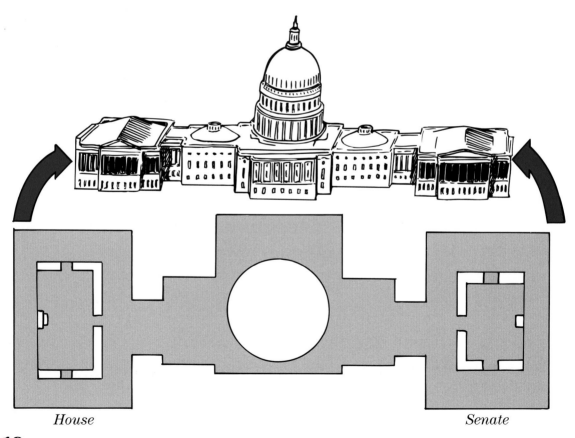

House   *Senate*

states had more representatives and therefore had more votes in the House; smaller states had fewer representatives and therefore had fewer votes.

To keep one branch from becoming more powerful than the others, the Framers wrote rules in the Constitution that gave each branch some power to control the power of other branches. These rules were called *checks and balances*. For example, the Constitution gave Congress the power to make laws, but it also gave the other branches power to check and balance Congress's power. It gave the president the power to stop a law by refusing to sign it. This power was called a *veto*. It gave the courts the power to review laws and to decide whether they are proper under the Constitution.

The People's Rights

When the Framers finished writing the Constitution, most of them believed they had developed a balanced system of government. They had created a new government from scratch and decided what power to give it. No nation had ever done that before.

But something was still missing. The Constitution did not say much about the rights of the people. Individual rights were

important to the people of the United States. They had fought the War of Independence to protect their basic rights from King George III and the British government. The British made the colonists pay taxes and obey other laws, even though the colonies did not help to make the laws. The British could arrest colonists who protested against the king and put them in jail without a fair trial. The king sent soldiers to enforce the laws and forced the colonists to let the soldiers live in their homes.

Some Framers were afraid that the new U.S. government, even with its checks and balances, could become too powerful. They wanted the Constitution to state what rights the people had and to say that the government could not take those rights away. Several states already wrote bills of rights into their constitutions to protect the people's rights from the state government. Some Framers wanted a bill of rights in the U.S. Constitution to protect the people's rights from the national government.

Elbridge Gerry, a wealthy merchant from Massachusetts, and George Mason, a planter and elder statesman from Virginia, argued for a bill of rights. Gerry and Mason were unhappy about other parts of the Constitution. In the convention's final days, Mason

Elbridge Gerry

argued that many people would fear that the Constitution gave too much power to the national government. Mason, who had written Virginia's Declaration of Rights, said a bill of rights would quiet those fears. Gerry, who had signed the Declaration of Independence, asked the convention to add a bill of rights to the Constitution.

George Mason

But the other Framers refused. The convention voted against adding a bill of rights. Why would so many great leaders, who had fought the British to protect rights such as free speech and fair trials, decide not to protect those rights in the Constitution?

One reason was that most of them did not think a bill of rights was necessary. They believed that the people kept all of their rights that the Constitution did not give to the government. Some Framers thought it would be impossible to list all of the people's rights. What would happen, they asked, to rights that were not listed in the Constitution? Would those rights still be protected?

The Framers also may have had other reasons for voting against a bill of rights. Many of them were tired. The bill of

rights came up in September, and the Framers had been meeting since May. Cold weather and winter were coming, and the men wanted to go home. Some may have feared that Gerry and Mason were trying to delay the convention so they could get other changes to the Constitution. They knew the Constitution was not perfect, but they also knew that the Constitution allowed Congress and the states to make changes, called *amendments*. If the people wanted a bill of rights, they could add one by amending the Constitution later.

The Constitutional Convention approved the Constitution without a bill of rights. Thirty-six Framers signed it on

September 17, 1787. Gerry and Mason, along with Edmund Randolph of Virginia who continued to have other disagreements with the Constitution, refused to sign.

Approving the Constitution

After the Framers were finished with their work, the states had to decide whether to approve the Constitution. The Constitution said that when conventions in nine states had approved the Constitution, it could take effect.

One by one, the states held conventions. People took sides. Those who were for the Constitution were called *Federalists*. Those who were against it were called *Anti-Federalists*.

As Gerry and Mason had predicted, one of the main arguments against the Constitution was that it did not have a bill of rights. Anti-Federalists at many state conventions said they would not approve the Constitution unless it said more about the people's rights. The author of the Declaration of Independence, Thomas Jefferson, wrote from France to his friend James Madison saying he was concerned that the Constitution did not have a bill of rights.

Nonetheless, several states approved the Constitution quickly. Then came a long debate in the Massachusetts convention. Massachusetts finally approved, but only after another compromise. The Massachusetts convention sent recommendations to Congress for nine amendments, including amendments to protect people's rights.

On June 21, 1788, New Hampshire became the ninth state to approve the Constitution, but their convention also recommended several amendments to protect individual rights. The United States was now a nation. But the Constitution and the new U.S. government could not succeed without two big states—Virginia and New York.

George Mason and Patrick Henry, who gave the famous "give me liberty or give me death" speech in the pre-Revolution days, led the Anti-Federalists in Virginia. James Madison led the Federalists. Mason's active opposition to the Constitution probably cost him his friendship with his longtime friend and neighbor, George Washington.

After several weeks of debate, the Virginia convention approved the Constitution, but it also recommended a Declaration of Rights. A month later, the New York convention approved, also recommending several amendments.

Adding the Bill of Rights

Madison still did not think a bill of rights was necessary to protect people's rights, but he was, however, a smart politician. He knew it was time for one more compromise. If the new U.S. government was going to succeed, the Constitution needed a bill of rights.

The first Congress took office in 1789. Madison was the leader of the Virginia delegation. He quickly wrote several amendments to the Constitution to protect people's rights and submitted them to Congress. They were based on rights protected in several of the state constitutions.

The new Congress soon approved Madison's amendments and sent them to the states for approval. By 1791, the states had approved ten of them. Those first ten amendments are called the Bill of Rights. They protect important rights that the states fought for in the Revolution. They continue to guard our rights today. Here is what they say.

First Amendment—Freedom of Religion, Freedom of Speech, Freedom of the Press, Freedom of Assembly, and Freedom to Petition

Many settlers had come to the colonies so they could practice their religion. In England and in other countries, people were sometimes punished and even thrown in jail if they did not practice their country's "official" religion. The First Amendment protects freedom of religion. It gives people the right to practice any religion—or no religion. It says the government cannot establish an official religion.

The First Amendment also protects the right to speak and write freely, even if the government does not like what someone says. The British had arrested people for giving speeches or writing articles that disagreed with the king. Our system of government, however, depends on people speaking out with different points of view and making compromises. The right of free speech is one of the most important rights.

Even today, in many countries, people are afraid to complain about their government. They might get beaten, thrown in jail, or killed. In the United States, however, we can usually say what we think in speeches, books, newspapers, movies, and on television without being punished. We can gather in large groups to protest

the government, as long as we protest peacefully. We can *petition* or tell the government what we want. The First Amendment protects all of these rights.

Second Amendment—Right to Keep and Bear Arms

Many people owned guns in colonial times. Colonists kept weapons so they could quickly form armies of citizen-soldiers, called militias, to protect their colonies when necessary. The British and French had fought a war in North America during the 1700s, and many battles were fought in or near the colonies. When the king sent soldiers to the colonies to enforce the tax laws, the colonists wanted to protect themselves from the British.

After the Revolutionary War, the people wanted to maintain the right to form militias when necessary to protect themselves. The Second Amendment declared that because militias were necessary to protect the states, the people had the right to own weapons. Today, even though states have National Guard troops that serve as militias, the Second Amendment still protects the right to own guns.

Third Amendment—Right Not to Quarter Soldiers

The Third Amendment restricts the government from forcing people to let soldiers stay in their homes. This was an important right to people who lived during the Revolution. When British soldiers occupied the colonies, they forced colonists to provide housing or *quarters* for them. Sometimes, this meant the colonists had to let the soldiers live in their homes. The colonists did not like this.

Since then, quartering soldiers has rarely been a problem in this country. The Third Amendment still states that the government cannot force us to let soldiers live in our homes during peacetime. It allows the government to put soldiers into private homes during a war, but only if the government makes laws for that purpose.

Fourth Amendment—Protection from Unreasonable Searches and Seizures

The people were particularly worried about protecting themselves and their property from a cruel government. They remembered how British soldiers came into colonists' homes, arrested them without a reason, seized their property, and kept them in jail for a long time. The British sometimes held trials far away, or in secret, so family and friends and people who could help the accused person could not attend. The people wanted protection against the new U.S. government from doing such things to them. So several amendments contained rules to protect the rights of people who were accused of crimes.

The Fourth Amendment says that the government needs a good reason to think someone broke the law before it can search or arrest them. It requires government officials to get written permission from a judge before searching someone or their property.

Today, thanks to the Fourth Amendment, if the police think you took someone's bicycle, they have to convince the judge that you probably took that bicycle before they can search your house for it. Police cannot arrest you, your friends, and everyone in the neighborhood hoping that someone admits to taking the bike. They have to convince the judge that they know who probably took the bike before they can make an arrest.

Fifth Amendment—Guarantees Due Process of Law and Protection from Testifying Against Yourself

The Fifth Amendment says the government cannot restrict someone's "life, liberty, or property" unless it follows "due process of law." *Due process* means the government must follow certain rules so that trials and other legal actions are fair. The Fifth Amendment provides some of these rules.

For example, if the government thinks you committed a crime, it must convince a group of people called a *grand jury* that you broke

the law before it can put you on trial. If you go on trial and the court decides that you are not guilty, then the government cannot put you on trial for that same crime again. The government also cannot force you to do or say anything that will prove you are guilty.

The Fifth Amendment also says the government cannot take someone's property unless it pays a fair price for it. For example, if your family owns land where the government plans to build a highway, the government can take the land only if it pays your family a fair price.

Sixth Amendment—Right to Fair, Speedy, Public Trial by Jury

The Sixth Amendment contains rules to ensure that people who are accused of crimes receive fair trials. These rules prevent the government from putting people in jail for a long time without a trial. They require the government to give people a fair chance to defend themselves.

Under the Sixth Amendment, the government must hold a trial quickly if it accuses you of committing a crime. The government must say what law you broke and must hold the trial in public. You have the right for a group of regular people from your community, called a *jury*, to decide whether you are guilty.

The Sixth Amendment also protects your right as the accused to listen to the people, called *witnesses*, whom the government brings to court to describe what you did. You have the right to ask the government's witnesses questions and to bring witnesses to court to tell your side of the story. The Sixth Amendment also protects your right to have a lawyer help defend you, even if the government has to pay for that lawyer.

Seventh Amendment—Right to Jury Trial in Cases That Are Not Crimes

The right to a jury trial was one of the few individual rights the Framers protected in the original Constitution. The Framers remembered how British judges who were loyal to the king could decide cases against the colonists. They wanted the right to have a jury decide whether they committed a crime. The Constitution said: "The trial of all Crimes . . . shall be by Jury." It said nothing, however, about juries in cases that were not crimes.

The Seventh Amendment expands the right to jury trials. It says that if people go to court to settle a disagreement, they can request a jury to decide the case if enough money is at stake. Many people who bring cases to court today request jury trials.

Eighth Amendment—Right to Bail and No Cruel or Unusual Punishments

The Eighth Amendment protects the right of people accused of crimes to get out of jail before trial. People accused of crimes can get out of jail if they give the government money, called *bail*, which the government keeps until trial. The government gives bail money back to the accused person when the person returns to court for trial. The courts decide how much bail to charge. The Eighth Amendment said the amount of bail must not be too much.

The Eighth Amendment also protects people who break the law from cruel or unusual punishments. In addition, it says the government cannot charge people overly large amounts of money, called *fines*, for breaking the law.

Ninth Amendment—Rights of the People

One reason the Framers did not include a bill of rights in the original Constitution was they were afraid that rights that were not mentioned would not be protected. The Ninth Amendment handles that problem. It protects rights that are not listed in the Constitution. It says that just because the Constitution mentions some rights, but not others, does not mean the people do not have rights that are not mentioned.

For example, the Constitution says nothing about the right to decide what college to go to or what kind of job to do. The Ninth Amendment means that people have many rights that are not mentioned in the Constitution.

Tenth Amendment—Rights of the States

The Framers wrote the Constitution to be "the supreme Law of the Land." State governments still had many powers, but the Constitution gave the U.S. government power over the state governments.

Many people worried about how much power the Constitution gave to the national government. They wanted the Constitution to say more about states' rights.

The Tenth Amendment says state governments have all powers that the Constitution does not either give to the U.S. government or take away from the states. For example, the Constitution says that only the U.S. government can make coins and paper money. That means states cannot print their own money. But the Constitution says nothing about what kind of schools the states can establish. So each state makes rules for its own schools.

Conclusion

The Framers who wrote the Constitution created a national government that shared power with the state governments. They made compromises so that neither small states nor large states would have too much power. They made more compromises to balance power among different parts of the government.

The Constitution, however, said very little about important individual rights that colonists had fought to protect in the war against the British. This worried many people. Leaders of several states recommended changes, called amendments, to the Constitution to protect the people's rights. Congress and the states added ten amendments to protect certain rights, and these

amendments became known as the Bill of Rights. More than 200 years later, we still have these rights.

"It's a free country" is more than a phrase. It means that we have many freedoms in this country, thanks to the Bill of Rights.

Glossary

Amendment
A change to the Constitution.

Anti-Federalists
People who were against the Constitution.

Bail
Money that people accused of crimes give to the government to hold to ensure that they will show up in court.

Bill of Rights
The first ten amendments to the Constitution of the United States. They protect many important rights of the people.

Branches
The different parts of the government. The U.S. government has three branches.

Checks and Balances
Rules that give each branch of government some power to control the power of the other branches.

Compromise
A deal in which one side gets some, but not all, of what it wants, and the other side gets some, but not all, of what it wants.

Confederation

A group or organization, such as a league. After the states became independent from Great Britain, they organized themselves into a confederation.

Constitution of the United States

The rules that establish the U.S. government and tell the government what its jobs are.

Constitutional Convention

The meeting in Philadelphia during the summer of 1787 at which the Framers wrote the Constitution of the United States.

Due Process

The requirement in the Constitution that the government must follow certain rules so that trials and other legal actions are fair.

Executive Branch

The branch of the government that is led by the President of the United States. The Constitution gives it the power to carry out and enforce the laws.

Federalism

The system of shared power between the state governments and the national government.

Federalists

People who supported the Constitution.

Fines

Money that people pay to the government as punishment for breaking the law.

Framers or Founders

The people who either wrote the Constitution of the United States or signed the Declaration of Independence. A few did both.

Grand Jury

If the government believes that someone committed a crime, they must convince a group of people called a grand jury before they can put the person on trial.

Houses

The two parts of Congress.

House of Representatives

The house of Congress in which the number of members from each state depends on how many people live in the state.

Judicial Branch

The part of the U.S. government that contains the courts. The Constitution gives it the power to decide whether laws meet the Constitution's requirements and to decide whether someone has broken the law and how to punish people who have.

Jury

A group of regular people who decide whether someone accused of a crime is guilty.

Laws
The rules that a government makes. Laws tell the people and the government what they can and cannot do.

Legislative Branch
The part of the U.S. government called the Congress. The Constitution gives it the power to make laws for the government and for the people.

Militia
An army of citizen-soldiers who come together when needed to protect their state.

National Government
A central government for all of the states in a country.

Petition
The right of the people to tell the government what they want.

Plantations
Large farms in the southern states on which slaves worked.

Quarters
Places for soldiers to live.

Representatives
People who are selected to make laws or decisions on behalf of someone else. For example, the people of the United States elect representatives to make laws for them in Congress.

Rights

The freedom to do, or not do, certain things, such as freedom of speech, freedom of religion, freedom from arrest without cause.

Senate

The house of Congress that has two members from each state.

Separation of Powers

The system of government that gives some power to each branch of government.

Slave Trade

The shipment of Africans to North America where they were bought and sold to work as slaves.

State

A place that has its own independent government.

Veto

The power of the President to stop a law from going into effect by not signing it.

Witnesses

People who go to court to tell their story for one side or the other.

Selected Bibliography

Many fine children's books provide additional information on the Bill of Rights. Here are some of them.

Burgan, Michael, *The Bill of Rights* (Compass Point Books, Mankato, MN, 2002).

Fritz, Jean, *Shh! We're Writing the Constitution* (The Putnam Publishing Group, New York, 1987).

Hauptly, Denis J., *"A Convention of Delegates": The Creation of the Constitution* (Atheneum, New York, 1987).

Hoff Oberlin, Loriann, *The Everything American History Book* (Adams Media, Avon, MA, 2001).

Krull, Kathleen, *A Kids' Guide to America's Bill of Rights: Curfews, Censorship, and the 100-Pound Giant* (Avon Books, New York, 1999).

Quiri, Patricia Ryon, *The Bill of Rights* (Children's Press, New York, 1998).

Swain, Gwenyth, *Declaring Freedom: A Look at the Declaration of Independence, the Bill of Rights, and the Constitution* (Lerner Publishing Group, Minneapolis, MN, 2004).

Yero, Judith Lloyd, *The Bill of Rights* (National Geographic Children's Books, Washington, DC 2004).

Index

●●